D0898829

The Selected Poems of

Shuntarō Tanikawa

Translated from the Japanese by

Harold Wright

NORTH POINT PRESS
San Francisco 1983

The original versions of these poems appeared in the following collections: *Tanikawa Shuntarō Shishū*, Shichosha, Tokyo, 1965; *Tanikawa Shuntarō Shishū Zoku*, Shichosha, Tokyo, 1979; *Shinsen Tanikawa Shuntarō Shishū*, Shichosha, Tokyo, 1977; *Sonohoka Ni*, Shueisha, Tokyo, 1979; *Kokakōra Ressun*, Shichosha, Tokyo, 1980. Some of the translations appeared in *Asia, K'uei Ksing: A Repository of Asian Literature* (Indiana University Press), *Mademoiselle, The New York Quarterly, The Poetry of Postwar Japan* (University of Iowa Press), *Sumac, Three Japanese Poets* (Sadler Recording Service), and *Triquarterly*.

Acknowledgments are due the International Literature and Arts Program (formerly the Asian Literature Program), directed by Bonnie R. Crown, for support for translations and for sponsoring a number of programs featuring readings of some of the translations contained in this book.

021846

12 50

Contents

The Poems

Twenty Billion Light Years of Loneliness

Growth

age three
there was no past for me

age five
my past went back to yesterday

age seven
my past went back to topknotted samurai

age eleven
my past went back to dinosaurs

age fourteen
my past agreed with the texts at school

age sixteen
I look at the infinity of my past with fear

age eighteen
I know not a thing about time

On Destiny

Lined up on a station platform
grade school children
grade school children
grade school children
grade school children
talking, playing, eating.

"Aren't they cute."
"Remember?"
Lined up on a station platform
grown ups
grown ups
grown ups
grown ups
looking, talking, longing.

"Just fifty years and fifty billion kilometers."
"Remember?"
Lined up on a station platform
angels
angels
angels
angels
silent and watching
silent and glowing.

Painting

across a seemingly uncrossable river
there was a seemingly unclimbable mountain

beyond the mountain something like a sea
beyond the sea something like a town

clouds are dark—
is fantasy a sin

within a white frame
there is such a painting

Sadness

There where the sound of waves
    of the blue sky is heard
it seems as if I'd come away
leaving some unimaginable thing.

At a station clearly in the past
I stood at a window for lost articles
and felt much sadder than before.

Spring

over cherry blossoms
white clouds
over clouds
the deep sky

over cherry blossoms
over clouds
over the sky
I can climb on forever

once in spring
I with god
had a quiet talk.

Museum

stone axes and the like
lie quietly beyond the glass

constellations rotate endlessly
many of us become extinct
many of us appear

then
comets endlessly miss collision
lots of dishes and the like are broken
Eskimo dogs walk over the South Pole
great tombs are built both east and west
books of poems are often dedicated
recently
the atom's being smashed to bits
the daughter of a president is singing
such things as these
have been happening

stone axes and the like
lie absurdly quiet beyond the glass

Twenty Billion Light Years of Loneliness

Mankind on a little globe
Sleeps, awakes and works
Wishing at times to be friends with Mars.

Martians on a little globe
Are probably doing something; I don't know what
(Maybe *sleep-sleeping*, *wear-wearing*, or *fret-fretting*)
While wishing at times to be friends with Earth
This is a fact I'm sure of.

This thing called universal gravitation
Is the power of loneliness pulling together.

The universe is distorted
So all join in desire.

The universe goes on expanding
So all feel uneasy.

At the loneliness of twenty billion light years
Without thinking, I sneezed.

Nero

(to a loved little dog)

Nero
another summer is coming soon
your tongue
your eyes
your napping in the afternoon
now clearly live again before me.

You knew but about two summers
I already know eighteen summers
and now I can remember various summers
        both of my own and not my own:
the summer of Maisons-Lafitte
the summer of Yodo
the summer of the Williamsburg Bridge
the summer of Oran
so I am wondering
about the number of summers
        that humanity has known.

Nero
another summer is coming soon
but it's not a summer when you were here
a different summer
a completely different summer.
A new summer is coming
I'll be learning various new things
beautiful things   ugly things
things to cheer me   things to sadden me

and so I ask—
what is it?
why is it?
what must be done?

Nero
you have died
without anyone being aware
     you have gone far away alone
your voice
your touch
and even your feelings
now clearly live again before me.

But Nero
another summer is coming soon
a new infinitely vast summer is coming
and then
I'll probably be walking on
to meet the new summer
     to meet autumn
          to meet winter
to meet spring   and
     to expect a new summer again
in order to know all the new things
and
in order to answer
     all my questions
          myself.

Sixty-two Sonnets

Sonnet 13: Now

The gleaming may glow on anything
All will kindly forget me
Living Now
The times I limitlessly love Now.

In midst of song that is always silent
At a too faint indication of god
Suddenly I am aware of Now—
Simply amid the quiet vastness.

The times I trust the abundance of Now
Here on this star and knowing death
I am free.

The passions may appease anything
Like the sun, like the sky,
Under these things that glow
        overflowing in silence.

Sonnet 16: Morning (No. 3)

The light was on all night
At dawn a letter arrived
The sky was lazy
Children were still asleep.

I get up
I throw away
I pick up
Then I become busy.

People begin to walk
I begin to forget
God begins to cry.

At night everything probably disappears
It was a sudden premonition
And at that time
      suddenly the sun began to shine.

Sonnet 45

When the wind is strong
The earth resembles someone's kite;
Even during the full noon hours
People feel that night is already there.

The wind is without words,
It merely whirls around and frets.
I think of wind on another star
Wondering if they can form a friendship.

On earth there is nighttime and the day
What do other stars do during these times?
How can they bear to spread in silence?

By day the blue sky is telling lies
While night mutters the truth, we sleep
And when morning comes we say we've dreamed.

Sonnet 56

Isn't the world a little star in absence?
Nightfall . . .
The world loiters as if it were lost
As though quite ashamed of itself.

On a time such as this
I gather little names
When once
I was lacking in words.

Occasionally sounds invoke the world
Move more clearly than my song:
Distant steam whistles   howling of dogs
        raindoors and sound of cutting.

These times the world secretly like twilight
Is listening to them
As if by these individual sounds
        makes certain of itself.

Sonnet 58

Because of remoteness
Mountains can become mountains,
When stared at too closely
A mountain comes to resemble myself.

Vast landscapes bring men to a halt,
Then men become aware of being surrounded
              by profuse remotenesses,
They are always
Remotenesses that make men men.

Yet, man inside himself
Possesses a remoteness
Therefore man continues on to yearn . . .

Occasionally man cannot exceed the place
              that transgresses every remoteness,
Without being seen anymore
Man at such times becomes the landscape.

Sonnet 62

The world loves me
(in cruel ways and at times
in gentle ways)
So I can always be alone.

Even the first time a girl gave herself to me
I merely listened to sounds of the world,
For me only simple sadnesses and joys were clear
Since I'm always a part of the world.

To the sky, to trees, to her
I fling myself
To become the very abundance of the world.

. . . I call her
And the world looks around
Then I am gone.

Concerning Love

Love

for Paul Klee

Forever
for so long, forever
bound for so far
for so long, for so far, joined together
for sake of the weak
for sake of those in love but separate
or those who live alone
forever
for so long, forever, we need unending song
so heaven and earth will not quarrel
so the separate will be joined again
for the return of a single heart to the people's heart
and trenches to ancient villages
and the sky to innocent birds
and fairy tales to little children
and honey to the diligent bee
and the world to the things without names
for so far
for so long, for so far, joined together
as if about to end itself completely
as if about to perfect itself completely
forever like the blueprint of god
for so long, forever, approaching perfection
so all can be joined together
so all separate things will cease to be
so all can continue to live under one name:
the tree and the woodcutter
the young girl and blood

the window and love
the song and another song
so that quarreling is over
to end the useless things for sake of life
in such plentifulness
for so long, forever, that image spreads
as if to have the world become the imitator,
the image that beckons with a gentle glance.

Billy the Kid

First a little dirt on my mouth and slowly big clods
of earth between my legs and over my gut   an ant whose
nest was smashed crawls quietly over my closed eyelids   the
folks have stopped crying and seem to be feeling good in the
sweat of their shoveling   in my chest there's two holes drilled
by a soft-eyed sheriff   my blood spurted from the two paths of
escape   then I really realized that blood wasn't mine   I
knew that my blood, me and my blood, was headed on back   above
me the only enemy I ever had   the dry blue sky   it's taken
everything from me   even on the run   even as I shot   even
while loving it, the blue sky that kept taking from me, in the end,
failed to take from me only one time   the time of my death   now
I have nothing to be taken from me   now at last I don't fear the
blue sky   I don't fear that silence or that endless blue   since
now I'm being taken away by the ground   I can go back to where I
can't be reached by the hands of the blue sky, to where I can live
without fighting   now my cries will be answered   now the
sounds of my gun will linger in my ears   now when I can no longer
hear or can no longer shoot.

In killing, I tried to make sure of men and myself   my
youthful way of proving was studded in colors of blood   but with
the blood of other men I couldn't paint away the blue sky   I
needed my own blood   I got it today   I made sure my own blood
clouded over the blue sky and then returned to the ground   so
now I can no longer see the blue sky or even remember it   I
smell the smell of my ground, now I am waiting to become the
ground   above me the wind is blowing   I no longer envy the
wind   soon I will become the wind   then soon without even

knowing the blue sky I will live in the blue sky   I'll become
a lone star   and know all the nights   and know all the
days   still turning around and around as a star.

Concerning a Girl

from a little basket on the kitchen shelf   I was about to
pick a star   the girl insisted she didn't care about a
harvest   I thought I had planted a seed but perhaps we too
had been planted seeds   without realizing it we were raised
and ripened and will probably wither away   later we're nothing
more than a tiny clod of earth in the middle of the world's
garden   yet this time we are the ones that will raise   someone
will stand on us and grope for a star with a huge hand   perhaps
even check for ripeness   however we are not fertilizer for
stars   even at that time a girl wise beyond doubt will be there
to plant her naked feet within us   then she herself will become
a flower   and when ripe   a star will naturally fall   the
flower knows all about this   and so will not be afraid of
dying   when standing on my tiptoes about to pick a star   I
was called by the girl

Picnic to the Earth

here let's jump rope together   here
here let's eat balls of rice together
here let me love you
your eyes reflect the blueness of sky
your back will be stained a wormwood green
here let's learn the constellations together

from here let's dream of every distant thing
here let's gather low-tide shells,
from the sea of sky at dawn
let's bring back little starfish
at breakfast we will toss them out
let the night be drawn away
here I'll keep saying, "I am back"
while you repeat, "Welcome home"
here let's come again and again
here let's drink hot tea
here let's sit together for awhile
let's be blown by the cooling breeze.

Concerning Love

I am I being stared at
I am I being doubted
I am I being looked back at
I am I being lost sight of
and I am not love.

I am flesh fleeing from the heart
feet that don't know the ground
hands that can't fling away the heart
eyes being stared at by a heart
and I am not love.

I am noon of a sunset
drama that's been choreographed
love murmers that are named
darkness grown too used to
and I am not love.

I am unknown sadness
joy that is staring
one that is chosen of joined things
unhappiness outside of happiness
and I am not love.

I am a most gentle glance
I am too much understanding
I am an erected penis
I am a ceaseless yearning
and yet I am not love.

Cycle of Months (Menstruation)

    1
within her someone prepares a banquet
within her someone carves an unknown son
within her someone is wounded

    2
the palm of god,
injured clumsily in the act of creation,
still finds it difficult to forget

    3
"with such accurate regularity   florid
funerals occur within me   they are
mourned in the color of celebration   they
continue, unwounded and unable to die, to
return to nothingness   my children who
are overly young . . . a ripe moon is
falling   there is no one to receive it
I am waiting   I am alone squatting
in a chilly place and waiting—
for someone to sow the moon
for someone to deprive me of this rising tide—
with a wound, lost to the memory
of all, within me that is outside the
reach of healing"

    4
. . . while alluring those who will to live

towards the shore   the tide flows full
within her   there within her lies a sea
calling to the moon   and as the moon
revolves around   there lies within her an
endless calendar . . .

Back

Here everyone is all arranged, but someone will probably die
sometime   and someone will probably be born sometime so
always someone is missing   when someone is missing we feel
uneasiness deep in our hearts   the blue sky, isn't it the
inside of someone's tossed-off undershirt?   isn't the sun
a blown out and forgotten flame?   no one lacks another
person   because we are all arranged   everyone can feel
the cold to his back   isn't there someone who really knows
this back of mine?   isn't there another person to let me know
that my back is somehow like it is   although everyone trusts
their own hands   although we feel the backs of one
another   although we can put our backs back to back and
warm them.

Evening

For the sake of night that meets the dead
there remains today a single evening;
in the faint darkness
suddenly the neck of a turning girl.

For the sake of tomorrow for the poor
there remains today a single evening;
holding hands
and going home,
        children are singing.

Concerning a Room

man has surrounded himself
space was too frightening
time has been too sad

then man felt safe
there instead of infinite space there were pure white walls
instead of infinite time there was a soft bed

yet doors and windows were needed
doors for close friends
windows for the beautiful summer sun

during the day the outdoors has blue sky and rain cloud walls
and a bed of fields and roads
however at night   man shuts himself in

"a beloved room" is something men have always muttered
the sky has faithfully had man live in close co-ordinates
spring   summer   autumn   winter   until suddenly on
                                                                [a day of death—

I don't know about man after that
but without him a room
gradually starts resembling the universe

Picture Book

Giving Life

gives life
June lilies give me life
dead fish gives life
a puppy wet with rain
sunset of that day gives me life
gives life
unforgettable memories give life
the god of death gives life
gives life
one face suddenly turned around gives me life
love is a blind snake
a twisted umbilical cord
a red-rusted chain
a paw of a puppy

This Day

something began for me that day
something ended for me that day
that day everyone was silent
soft sunlight shone on maple leaves
angels were yawning that day
a day like today
a day like yesterday
nothing began for anyone else that day
nothing ended for anyone else that day
alone I crossed a railroad crossing
and crossed back over again
and crossed again
I then crouched in the middle of the tracks
and looked down the tracks at the setting sun

that was a day like today
a day like tomorrow
I kept quiet, unable to weep this day
somebody moves around in the womb
something begins for me this day
something ends for me this day
pods of peas are snapped
a kitten falls into the river this day
a day of death amid life

Hands

hands
they feel
hips of women
hands
they tease
hair of boys

hands
they squeeze
hammers
hands of friends
hands
they seize
daggers
hemlines of lives

hands
they strike
a father's face
hands
they stroke
inkslabs

hands
they create
they destroy
they take
hands

they give
they hold
hands
they release
they open
hands
they close
hands

ceaselessly do something
ceaselessly do nothing

hands
they indicate in vain
thickly luxuriantly
    like leaves in summer

hands
wide open they wither

Everyone

Everyone possesses something sad
and hides it in silence from everyone.
ha ha ha
Everyone possesses something unforgivable
keeping it possessed without forgiveness.
ha ha ha
At night   before going to bed
everyone has one look of sadness
like a rabbit or a snake
a look that sees nothing at all.
ha ha ha
Everyone possesses something unspeakable
so without knowing what to say
he possesses it all alone.
ha ha ha ha ha ha ha ha ha
So sometimes suddenly
          he wants to do something
                    like kiss a girl
forcing her tongue down with his own
firmly for a long time
and then ruthlessly open his eyes
to look at the distant sky
          or in the direction of the hills.

August

August is a dreamless month
I saw
everywhere the blue sea
and thighs of sun tanned girls
I saw!
The sun shifting
the wind sweeping the shore
and then
my blood and the sea and the night
all took on the same smell.
Other than that there was nothing
other than that
there was
nothing
August
was filled with the glory of this star.

August and February

The boy put the puppy in a basket.
The boy put the puppy in a basket
               and weighted it down.
The boy was crying.
The cicadas were very noisy.

    The girl's room was cold;
    we were covered with many blankets.
    The girl's body smelled of dry grass.
    At dusk   sleet was falling.

The boy looked at the basket
               there on the river bank.
The puppy wagged its tail.
The sun was nearly scorching.

    In the dimness of the room
    we were soaked with sweat;
    then finally soundly went to sleep.

The boy shutting his eyes
               threw the basket into the river,
and then still crying he ran away.

    When we opened our eyes
    it was already dark outside.

The boy that night couldn't stop crying.

Child and Train Tracks

the child that day too was busy
busy with drawing train tracks
train tracks forever all over the street

the child was busy every day
the street went on forever
so the two lines of white chalk
continued forever without a terminal
the child was busy every day

meanwhile
without love and with love
people got off and on real trains

while the child drew train tracks
people leaned over their fences
laughing or else weeping
without love or with love

then one day
when the child was hit by a train
the setting sun just like a terminal
was suspended beyond the white chalk tracks

Sky

For how long does the sky extend?
For how far does the sky extend?
For the duration of our lives,
How does the sky endure its blueness?

Even beyond our deaths,
Does the sky keep extending?
Below is a waltz resounding?
Below do poets doubt the sky's blueness?

Today children are busy at play;
Thousands of "scissors, paper, stones"
    are thrown to the sky.
Turning jumpropes tirelessly measure the sky.

Why is the sky so still about everything?
Why doesn't it say not to play?
Why doesn't it say to play?

Doesn't the blue sky wither away,
Even beyond our deaths?
If it doesn't truly wither away,
Why is the blue sky still?

For the duration of our lives,
Over towns or villages and seas,
Why does the sky
Go away alone in darkness?

Family

(Dialogue between a boy and his elder sister. "Imagine them out West, she's dressed in Gingham. . . ." Conversation with Tanikawa, Washington, D.C., April, 1970.)

Hey, sister.
Who is coming? Up to the loft?

We are coming.

Hey, sister.
What is ripening? On the stairs?

We are ripening, brother.
You and me and father and mother.
Outside the weather is dry.
We are working.

Who is going to eat?
The bread on the table?

We are going to eat,
tearing it with our nails.

Well then,
who is going to drink?
My sister's blood?

Oh, you don't know him.
He's tall and has a nice voice . . .

Hey, sister, Hey, sister.
What did you do in the barn?

We cast a spell,
so all of us won't die,
he and I cast a spell.

And then?

And then,
my breasts will grow full
for the sake of one more of us.

Who is that?

That is me, that is you,
that is father and mother.

Then who will come?
At night? When it's time
to say prayers?

No one.

Above the weathercock?

No one.

Beyond the dust of the road?

No one.

At dusk? Beside the well?

We are all here.

Sadness

Sadness
A half-peeled apple
Not a metaphor
Not a poem
Merely there
A half-peeled apple
Sadness
Merely there
Yesterday's evening paper
Merely there
Merely there
A warm breast
Merely there
Nightfall
Sadness
Apart from words
Apart from the heart
Merely here
The things of today.

Request

Turn inside out   turn me
Plow the fields inside me
Dry up the wells inside me
Turn inside out   turn me
Wash out my insides
And maybe you'll find a splendid pearl
Turn inside out   turn me
Is the inside of me the sea?
Is it the night
Is it a distant road
Is it a polyethylene bag
Turn inside out   turn me
What is growing inside of me
A field of overripe cactus plants?
A premature offspring of a unicorn?
A buckeye tree that failed to become a violin?
Turn inside out   turn me
Make the wind blow through me
Let my dreams catch cold
Turn inside out   turn me
Let my concepts weather away.

Turn inside out
Turn inside out please   turn me
Please shelter my skin
My forehead is frostbitten
My eyes are red with bashfulness
My lips are weary of kisses

Turn inside out
Turn inside out please turn me
Let my insides worship the sun
Spread my stomach and pancreas over the grass
Evaporate the reddened darkness!
Stuff the blue sky into my lungs!
With my spermaduct all entangled
Have me trampled by black stud horses
Please have my heart and brain,
                            using chopsticks of plain wood,
Be eaten by the one I love.

Turn inside out
Turn inside out please   turn me
Let all the words within me
Be chatted completely away   and quickly
Let the singing quartet of instruments
Be resounded completely away
Let the aged birds within me
Be flown completely away
Let the love within me
Be lost in an evil gambling den.

Turn inside out, please turn, inside out, turn me
I'll give away the fake pearl inside me
So turn inside out, please turn, inside out, turn me
Silence alone speaks softly within me
Let me depart
Outside of myself
To that shade of trees
Over that woman
Into that sand.

Silence

two people loving each other
hold each other in silence
love compared to words of love
is too small or   at times
too large
so two people loving each other
in order to be exact and precise
in loving each other
hold each other in silence
when they are silent
the blue sky is friendly
small stones are friendly
the soles of their naked feet
dirty with dust from the room
soil the bed sheets
the night slowly makes everything nameless
the sky is nameless
the room is nameless
the world is nameless
all are siblings of nameless existence
only God
due to the weight of that first name
with a thud
like a little lizard
falls between the two

Window

BANG   BANG!
The window banged in the wind.
BANG   BANG!
The clouded sky was an empty can.
BANG!   BANG!
Inside the window a man and woman
twisting and turning
like a rotten rope
twisting and turning
       yearning   loving   *l-o-v-e*!
BANG   BANG!
Inside my soul
       all the countless words
              like worms
squirmed in fright of that sound.
BANG   BANG!
That sound
that suffering
songless
senseless
speechless
sound.
BANG   BANG!
One window in the world
       clanking in the wind.
A man and woman enraptured
no one looks from the window.

Over and Over

Over and over and more over and over over and over   More and more
over and over over and over over and over   Over and over continuing
over and over more over and over over and over   How many times over
and over and over must it be done over and over   The words die over
and over die leaving over and over only the over and over   The occasions
of continuing the over and over over and over   The sun rises and
the sun sets and days are over and over over and over   The boiling
of rice over and over meets the morning over and over over and over and
the night over and over comes before we are aware.
Don't say, don't say the words good bye!
The happiness of separation is no one's at all.
We over and over do nothing more than over and over
dream over and over of each other holding
        each other and over and over drooling!
We are no longer meeting over and over
forever meeting over and over or not meeting
        over and over among those trees.
The wind is blowing.
Today over and over the unending sounds
of our coughs and water-filled cookpots
oh tomorrow tomorrow
how very far away you are.

August

King of kings
He is not here.
Ah, a beautiful summer!

Blood of blood
Does not flow for anyone.
Ah, a beautiful summer!

A girl is nude
A horse jumps over a rose
Ah, a beautiful summer!

Who? Who?
Sings for the sake of death
              (in a river voice)
Ah, a beautiful summer!

November

November
prohibited
I continue to live
prohibited
by only one
prohibited
by your gentle glances
November
children playing hide-and-seek
the sun over a persimmon tree
I try to pray but can't pray.

November
permitted
I continue to live
permitted
by songs that flow along the street
    also by sky
by half-built houses
    by neglected cats
November
children under the trees
permitted
I sit in a sunny place
permitted
wearing blue denims.

Night Jazz

Taro is blind
since it is night
Hanako too is blind
since it is night
nothing is seen
only touched
Taro touches
Hanako too touches
extremely lively fish
extremely fresh shellfish
extremely terrible storm
extremely rocking boat
extremely dark night
extremely extremely
extreme
quiet spreading of four branches
                               and four roots
at dawn
birds drop in
at dawn
the blue sky
but now
since it is night
Taro is blind
since it is night
Hanako too is blind
packed full of dreams
blindness

even two jars
even two chairs
even one house
even many towns
even one road
even a crying baby
in dreams
touched with blind eyes
a faint tomorrow
a cute pee pee of an angel
points to the future
aaah! eeee! oo! eh! ooh!
setting fire to the rear end of god.

Kiss

She came home smelling of another man,
and I just could not kiss her.
Then taking quilts still warm from the sun
we went to bed together.
It had been such nice weather that day;
still I could not kiss her.
She pressed her breasts firmly to my chest;
still I couldn't do it.
I felt she was a different girl,
as if we had never met.
Still without getting between her legs,
it seemed like a Sunday
        when I used to go fishing alone
and would watch the soft sun of winter
        beside that little pond.
It seemed like the times
        I used to wait to meet someone.
I was frightened—
Still I couldn't do it.
Then sometime I fell asleep.
The night was like a huge prairie
for as long as one could run,
        for as long as one could run.

Boy's March

peepee is pointed
like a rocket to the moon
fly, fly, peepee
while he who's "it" hides his eyes.

peepee is soft
like a tiny pet
run, run peepee
faster than Kiki the snake.

peepee is cold
a bud beginning to bloom
bloom, bloom, peepee
honey that fills up a jar.

peepee is hard
like the pistol of a thief
shoot, shoot, peepee
and kill all the soldiers of lead.

Question and Answer

becoming mutually mutual questions
and never arriving at answers
our words at last
drown in the wells of our individual hearts
when the world is a question
I alone answer
when I am a question
the world alone answers
poetry in the end is nothing but blood
stars keep revolving within desolation
conversation within me alone
remaining silent forever
can only ripen this way.

Face

Let the desert be the world's forehead
let the trees be the world's hair
the sky the pupils of the eyes
mountains the nose   fire the lips
let the seas be the cheeks of the world
let the world be a single face
make my blind eyes two moles
make my frozen heart a little earring
let the world become
one single fearfully smiling face.

Family Portrait

Filled with water
There's a jar
Eating of gruel begins
Wooden spoons
Berry wine
All is supported
By a heavy table.

There's a man
Wearing coarse cloth
Sitting
Strong arms
Fierce beard
Eyes fixed
In a gaze
At a field still dark.

There's a woman
Large breasts
Coiled-up hair
Hot hands
On the man's shoulders.

There's a child
His curved brow
Smeared with dirt
As if surprised
He turns around.

The old people
In a picture on the wall
Beside a calendar
Are gently waiting
A dog like a bear
Yawns by the door.

At a simple altar
A flame is glowing
The night is quietly
Beginning to dawn.

FROM

Lampoons

New Year's Vow

I vow not to stop drinking or smoking.
I vow to bathe those I dislike with vile language.
To look around at pretty girls.
I vow at times appropriate to laugh,
                        to laugh with a wide open mouth.
To gaze absentmindedly at sunsets.
To gawk at mob scenes.
I vow to doubt while weeping at heart-warming stories.
Not to have academic discussions about the world and country.
To write bad poems and good poems.
I vow not to give my opinions to newspaper reporters.
I vow not to buy a second T. V. set.
I vow not to want to ride in a space ship.
I vow not to regret breaking vows.
In witness whereof we sign.

Expulsion

Names may be eliminated from lists,
but people remain.
People may be eliminated,
but ideas remain.
Ideas may be eliminated,
but blind life remains.
Life has a dislike of death,
life shrieks over meaningless things,
life is certainly never eliminated.
Life has but one name:
"Gombei the nameless."*

*TANIKAWA: "Gombei" is a humorous, rural-sounding name often used in children's games. Perhaps like
"Mr. No-name or something."

Adult Time

A child in a week
becomes a week smarter.
A child in a week
learns fifty new words.
A child in a week
can bring change to himself.
An adult in a week
is the same as before.
An adult in a week
turns over the same weekly.
An adult takes a week
merely to scold a child.

Growth

Drawing a meaningless line,
a child says it's an apple.

Painting an apple just like an apple,
a painter says it's an apple.

Painting an apple unlike an apple,
an artist says it's truly an apple.

Not painting an apple or anything else
members of the Academy of Art
slurp up apple sauce.

Apples, apples, red apples,
are apples bitter? Are they sour?

To Steal

Honor can be stolen,
but pride can't be stolen.

Words can be stolen,
but poetry can't be stolen.

Houses can be stolen,
but the blue sky can't be stolen.

Clothes can be stolen,
but nudity can't be stolen.

A monarch can be stolen,
but the self cannot be stolen.

A Child

A child is still one more hope
even in this careworn world.

A child is still one more joy
even in midst of all our fear.

A child is still one more angel
however much we don't believe in god.

A child is still our reason
reason for living,
      reason for risking death.

A child is still one more child
even in arms of stone.

Concerning Obscenity

No matter how pornographic a movie
it can't be as obscene
        as a couple in love.
If love is something human
obscenity too is something human.
Lawrence, Miller, Rodin,
Picasso, Utamaro, the Manyō poets:
were they ever afraid of obscenity?
It is not a movie that is obscene
we are the ones basically obscene
warmly, gently, vigorously,
and with such ugliness and shame—
we are obscene
nights and days obscene
with nothing else, obscene.

For Free

Books have prices?
A Picasso several million?
Alimony for separated women?
Patent fees?
Copyright fees?
Getting royalties for writing poetry?
What barbarous customs!

The air, the sea, the Milky Way,
love, thought, song, and poems,
women, children, and friends:
Truly all important things
are FREE!
           . . . or ought to be.

Color

Hope is composed of complex colors:
the red of a betrayed heart
the ash color of days on end
the yellow of a fledgling's beak
mixed with the blueness of blues
the brownness of skin
with ardor of black magic
the golden dreams of alchemy
with flags of various nations
the green of virgin forests and, of course,
the seven embarrassed hues of the rainbow.

Hopelessness is a simple color:
a pure white.

Fantasy Statistics

BROKEN BRANCHES: Eight million six hundred twenty-one thousand and
[three.
INJURED BUTTERFLIES: Five hundred thirteen thousand four hundred and
[twenty-one.
BORN GENIUSES: Minus three.
UNTIED RIBBONS: Sixty-nine thousand five hundred and fifteen meters.
FLOWN TEARS: Five hundred and eight million cubic meters.
INNOCENT MEN: Zero.
SNEEZES: Incalculable.
FADED RAINBOWS: Just the number of men who have gotten married.
BROKEN KETTLEDRUMS: Four.
PLATONIC LOVE: 8½.
REGRETTABLE SITUATIONS: Infinitely large.
ME: Just one.

Miscellaneous Poems

Beggar

I was asked why I was silent;
it was just because there was no way to say it
        except by being silent.
They beat me,
broke my crutches,
and killed my little brown dog.
I laughed. So I am an eternal beggar,
and right before all the good citizens
I'll remain crouched
        and live on forever.

River

Mother,
Why is the river laughing?

Why, because the sun is tickling the river.

Mother,
Why is the river singing?

Because the skylark praised the river's voice.

Mother,
Why is the river cold?

It remembers being once loved by the snow.

Mother,
How old is the river?

It's the same age as the forever young springtime.

Mother,
Why does the river never rest?

Well, you see it's because the mother sea
is waiting for the river to come home.

Song of March

I go flinging away flowers
everything is budding
in March.

I go flinging away paths
children are scampering about
in March.

I go flinging away song
skylarks are singing
in March.

I go cmbracing only love
the pain and fear and
you—

Your laughter
in March.

Dog

Sadder than myself
there is a dog
there—
down the alley
silent
cowering
only his eyes are wide open
nobody calls him
nobody notices him
when I am sad
sadder than myself,
there is a dog
always
there
beside me
never begging for pity,
merely
there.

On a Beautiful Summer Morning

I want to become a giant
these mountains
these clouds
this blue sky
this summer morning
I want to hold in my arms.
I want to become a giant
the happiness beyond the mountains
I'd pluck with my fingers
to put in my pocket
and every yearning
over towards the night
I would snatch away
like little birds.
I want to become a giant
once a day a heart beat
eyes to gaze at eternity
fingertips to scorch the sun
to jot history in a diary
the misery of revolutions
the glory of betrayal
I'd scoop that all in my hands.
I want to become a giant
to fling myself into the darkness of the universe
to swim in the flowing Milky Way
to hold the earth in my arms

to silently shed tears
with unlimited helplessness
I want to become a giant.

But if that isn't possible at all
I want to become a single ant
to be always astray in a maze of dewy grass
to continue on forever astray
just that would be good
on this beautiful summer morning.

Stone and Light

The stone doesn't repel the light,
The stone doesn't absorb the light.
On the stone sits a deerfly,
The light is radiant in its downy hair.

The light just now arrived on earth.

Ten Yen Coin

With his last ten yen coin
the boy wanted to make a phone call.
He wanted to talk to someone close
        in a rowdy language,
but none of his friends had telephones.
The ten yen coin was wet in his palm
and smelled of metal.
(Why should I buy gum?
        This ten yen coin will be used
                for something more important.)
Then the boy saw the car,
a haughty car like a beautiful woman,
a fierce car like an unreachable happiness . . .
and before he knew it himself,
the boy, taking the ten yen coin in his hand,
        cut into that beautiful finish,
a long deep gash—
Then the boy threw the ten yen coin,
with all his might,
        into the city's congestion.

Bomb

The boy made a bomb;
it took a long time   alone.
He made a time bomb in the shed,
but there was no one to do in.

The boy wanted to explode the bomb;
he longed for the loud sound,
        the beautiful fireworks,
and to frighten the girls.
That was really all.

The boy going to a busy corner,
placed the bomb under a mailbox.
At a coffeehouse he drank warm milk
waiting, with beating heart, for that "time."

A pretty little girl led a pure white dog,
who finding the mailbox . . . peed,
and the gunpowder was completely soaked.

Two Tokyos

Withdrawing all his postal savings
and putting on his only suit,
he packed a bag with old newspapers
and went to a hotel with a foreign name.
He slept in a fluffy bed   (alone).
In the morning he ate oatmeal and melon,
in the afternoon he took three showers,
at night he took a sightseeing bus
          with a man from Peru.
TOKYO was noisy.
TOKYO was huge.
TOKYO was fancy.
He wanted to send a picture postcard somewhere,
but there was nowhere to send one.
So he wrote one to himself,
          addressing it to his rooming house,
saying, "Tokyo has everything."

When he returned to his rooming house
the post card was glittering on his bed.

Rain Please Fall

Rain please fall
over an unloved woman
rain please fall
in place of unflowing tears
rain please fall   secretly.

Rain please fall
over the cracked fields
rain please fall
over dried up wells
rain please fall   and soon.

Rain please fall
over the napalm flames
rain please fall
over the burning villages
rain please fall   furiously.

Rain please fall
over the endless desert
rain please fall
over hidden seeds
rain please fall   gently.

Rain please fall
over the reviving green

rain please fall
for sake of a glowing tomorrow
rain please fall   today.

Eleven Poems for Paul Klee

I Before the Snow

paper is white
paper is snow
paper is winter
painter is sun
melting the snow

painter is spring
painting is green
painter is summer
painting blue
painter is autumn
painting red
and then presently—

painter is standing
on new paper
on a horizon of snow

II   Child on the Steps

to the child on the steps
you cannot speak out
you can only weep
due to the child on the steps

to the child on the steps
you can give nothing
you can only die
for sake of the child on the steps

the child on the steps is alone
but he is nameless
so you cannot call out
you can only be called

III   Black King

the clear-bellied child
was sad since his belly was empty
the full-bellied king
was sad since his belly was full

the child heard the sound of the wind
the king heard music
tears appeared to the eyes of both
here on the same single star

IV   Kettledrummer

even the loudest sound
cannot disturb the silence
even the loudest sound
resounds through the silence

the chirping of birds
and the explosion of missiles
silence embraces both in those arms
silently forever in those arms

V   Stern Face

the stern man
sternly walks
it's sad

the stern man
sternly cries
it's funny

the stern man
sternly is sorry
it's irritating

the stern man
sternly kills
it's frightful

VI   Landscape with Yellow Birds

there are birds
so there is sky
there is sky
so there are balloons
there are balloons
so children are running
children are running
so there is laughter
there is laughter
so there is sadness
so there is prayer
and ground for kneeling
there is ground
so water is flowing
and there's today and tomorrow
there is a yellow bird
so with all colors forms and movements
there is the world

VII   Chosen Site

in going there
words stumble
in surpassing words
a soul gasps
yet before that soul
something like a faint light is seen
in going there
a dream explodes
in piercing dreams
darkness glows
yet before the picture's darkness
something like a large hole is seen

VIII   Puppet Show

you know you are manipulated
so you play around like that

strings are limp
strings are taut
strings are tangled

up to my manipulating fingertips
there comes along the strings
your very life—

you know you are manipulated
so at night you sleep
        as deep as that

IX   Fight Scene from the Comic Fantasy
Opera, "The Seafarer"

it was sometime somewhere
a fight actually occurred
no, it wasn't a dream
no, it wasn't a play
there at sea

you remember
that time before you were born
that place where you were not
and the screaming
at the overwhelming fear

towards another world
you cannot awake
you slide over slimy scales
into the fish-smelling mouth
and you're swallowed whole

X   Death and Fire

there is no one to die in place of me
so I must die myself
not the bones of anyone else
I'll become bones of my own
sadness
flowing of the river
the chatting of people
a spider web wet with morning dew
not a single one of these
can I take along with me
maybe one song I like at least
will be given to me to listen to
with my ears of bone

XI   The Golden Fish

the large fish with a large mouth
eats a middle-sized fish
the middle-sized fish
eats a little fish
the little fish
eats a smaller
fish
as life is sacrificed for life
light is glowing
happiness is nourished by unhappiness
flowers fertilize
even in the deepest joy of the sea
a single tear
must be said to be melting

Two Later Poems

Adherence to Apples

It can't be called red, it's not color but apple.
It can't be called round, it's not shape but apple.
It can't be called sour, it's not taste but apple.
It can't be called expensive, it's not price but
apple. It can't be called pretty, it's not beauty
but apple. It can't be classified, it's not a plant,
but because it's an apple.

Blooming apples. Ripening apples. Apples on branches
swaying in the wind. Rained upon apples, pecked
upon apples, picked off apples. Apples fallen upon
the ground. Rotten apples. Apple seeds, sprouting
apples. Apples useless to refer to as apples. Apples
that aren't apples, apples that are apples, apples that
are or aren't, simply one apple is all apples.

McIntosh, Delicious, Baldwin, Jonathan, Winesap, Northern Spy,
a single apple, three or five or a dozen
or seven kilos of apples, twelve tons
of apples or two million tons of apples. Production
of apples, transported apples. Measured, packaged,
bought and sold apples. Sterilized apples, digested
apples, consumed apples, vanished apples.
Apples! Apples?
That, that over there, that there. There
that there, that in a basket. That falling
from the table, that copied on canvas,
that baked in an oven. Children take it in their

the number eaten, despite the number rotten, they
spring one after another from branches, that which
gleamingly, endlessly, overflow shops. A replica of what?
A replica of when?

Unable to answer, they are apples. Unable to ask,
they are apples. Unable to tell, after all they are
apples, still . . .

Poem Written at 14 East 28 Street, New York City

Then, of course, to cash travelers checks
I wrote my name over and over;
take people as they are at present,
I wonder if they can be saved?

If they cannot be saved,
what can be done for men dying tonight?
If they can be saved,
what is the future good for?

If it's just my own soul to be saved
how easy it would be,
but I'm always being invaded by others' souls
so I can't see my own soul very well.

Then dawn arrives again,
I was awakened by a call from Tokyo;
I said, "Good morning."
My daughter and son said, "Good night."

Something Else

Lost Thing

I lost a very worthless thing
nothing I couldn't do without
nothing that held fond memories for me
nothing I couldn't get anew at the corner store
but only because I couldn't find it
every drawer became a perpetual maze
where I spent three hours in wandering,
bewildered, I went down to the garden
     and viewed the eastern sky.
Near the eave's edge as the first star was beginning to glow
I asked the reason that I lived,
an unconnected doubt that floated to my head.
Why, decades have passed since I pondered such a thing
of course, answers don't come that easily.
But to really look for something lost   .
     I could at least straighten up my clothes,
and with recollected courage reenter the room,
wondering if the familiar furnishings
     hadn't all expired in the glowing gloom.

Zoo

Bathed by tree filtered sun,
    my little girl rides a "monkey train"
when she comes closer I feel happy
when she goes away I feel sad
every third time around I failed pressing the shutter.

There are lots of families just like us
I don't feel happier than them
I don't feel less happy than them
yet, my mood slowly darkens.

The elephant raises and lowers its trunk
the crocodile continues to quietly exist
the deer leaps
what kind of animal can I be called?

Dog and Master

Lifting a leg at the base of a telephone pole
a dog urinates
at the end of a leather leash
a master waits patiently.

Stopping in front of a bookstore
a master stands reading
at the end of a leather leash
a dog waits patiently.

Linked by a leather leash, the two souls
are not immortal together
a dog smells the wind
what does a master smell?

A Laugher

A laugher's belly shakes
A laugher has a mouthful of cavities
A laugher makes some people mad, but
A laugher can't be told not to laugh
A laugher may be bad or good, but
A laugher and I are friends for now
A laugher keeps an embarrassed dog
A laugher too may cry at any time.

What Else

My little girl sobs on my lap
—what else am I waiting for?

In the distance a madrigal begins to be sung
a closed book
shade of a walnut tree

Words aren't good enough
words continue their calling
since they are never gratified

Silence isn't good enough
silence continues
since it is immortal

What else are we waiting for?
here on my lap
ending her sobbing, my little girl.

To You

To tell the truth that lipstick
would be better, I feel, wiped off
and that blue stuff on your eyelids.

The you you see is always the you in a mirror
the face of yourself you yourself see
still the real you lies outside a mirror.

Behind that you a river is flowing
over the face of that you a light is moving
it is that you that I watch.

What you yourself are
would be so hard to put into words
since there is probably nothing like you.

You who sit before me on a train
a pug-nosed you who grasps a rail pass
a button is loose on your smock!

Were I to say you were pretty
I'd have to be a hypocrite
still were I to say you were ugly,
      what would I have to be?

Moments when you are more beautiful
        than The Naked Maja
could be fantasized by me over and over
with apologies, of course, to Goya.

Porno-Bach

Are those fingers, the ones playing Bach just now,
and these fingers really the same?
This thing of mine, getting long and getting short,
and not resembling a piano at all,
must be called a comical tool;
so how does this conventional thing
and the great Bach, by your soft fingers,
get joined together?
I, myself, have no idea!
Yet, that thing of yours and this of mine,
now the color of the naked heart,
feel so warm, so smooth
in endless surrender much like death,
and when in this transparent blood filled darkness
I unexpectedly seem to meet Bach face to face.

Theresa

I remember Theresa
she entered a room
carrying nothing at all
along with a mere stirring of air.

Small cakes fill a dish
hot tea steeps in a bowl
forever bitterly reviled about who I am,
a wall has fallen away, a roof crumbles.

Covered by spores, eaten by maggots
a lifetime a wordless prolonged groan
each of my pores listens to that voice
having loved Theresa, all my dreams are denied.

Taste of plaster, taste of grapes mix on my tongue
after winds of October, frosts of November
I remember Theresa
even without having met.

A Sketch

All of us are already dead
in a thinly smoke shrouded forest
a crane-fly is caught in a spider's web
an electrical insulator lies fallen in the grass.

While decaying away I do recall
a woman's lips starting to part
      and in that inner darkness
a moving tongue.

Could it be that words were about to be spoken?
could it have been the start of a caress for me?
could it be a glass of water was wanted?
could it be that they eventually were all the same?

With my undeceiving eyes, ears, mouth and genitals
with these things I too wrote,
merely to savor without meaning.

Burned, charred, water-soaked,
a lump of book hardly retaining its shape
lies on mouldy leaves in dim sunlight
and even there time is still inscribed.

Sour enough to stab and spreading tartly
harshly sweet and blindingly bitter
it grows fainter, a strange fruit's memory.

Dusk

Once more drifting clouds gather in the western sky
while we, being sustained over and over by things over and over,
are still driven towards a tomorrow;
old melodies sung in faint memories are revived,
condolences for the dead deepen in the dimming afterglow,
is there anything that needs to be added to our world?
Comets depart for distances without attaining a single glance
along with many books and much music people grow old,
once more puppies snuggle to a mother dog's breast,
while we, being soothed over and over by things over and over,
still walk towards something which returns no more.

Coca Cola Lesson

Diary of Old Women

The old woman is seen squatting on a bank. Behind her smoke is spewing from a large chimney. You don't say do that to the old woman. You don't say do this. The old woman is an old woman. Tonight she says she'll boil some *konnyaku*.*

•

Forgetting what she has just said, the old woman repeats the same story. Thinking she is angry, you find she is cheerful the next moment. I used to be able to really cook rice in the old days, but look at the way it's burnt. Yet, it doesn't matter, the burning will soon be forgotten. What a shame! To burn something that way! The old woman absent-mindedly blames somebody else. Within the elusive old woman, the sincere old woman of the past plays hide-and-seek. Did the old woman go off somewhere? No, the old woman is there, still. With beautiful white hair shining in the sun, she lives.

•

Ah, leave it alone, the old woman said she said. The apron, getting caught on a broken nail, got torn. The man then jerked his hands away. That man is a bungler; the old woman is angry. Although it happened over thirty years ago, the old woman, with flairing nostrils, is really angry for awhile.

•

Visible old women are not of course the only old women. Old women corrode me like a virus. Invisible old women are more dangerous than visible old women, and I have stopped making distinctions between them and my-

*A paste made from the starch of the devil's tongue plant. Formed into cakes, it is a common food like *tofu*.

self. In order to have invisible old women become visible, I try to sketch old women. Immunity? Of what use is a word like that?

·

The old woman takes great care with the chipped tea stained pot. When she pours her coarse tea from that pot into a cup she is most magnificent. She then quietly looks at the newspaper, and knows quite well that the two events of an abandoned child and a coup d' etat, because they are joined together in the same size type, are of equal importance. She has lost three pairs of glasses for old people, these are her fourth.

·

Naming something clearly is not possible in this world of ours. Like a cookpot is made from a jumble of things that are not cookpots, sadness is the mere shadow of countless fearfully wearisome former things. One name is just like a black hole sucking into itself all other names. Names take root in the nameless. (Added as a note in haste.)

·

The world will get to be a better place says the old woman. But that's the way the world is, says the old woman. In the evening, with her face to the wall, the old woman cries. I have seen her. I can do nothing but go on watching over the old woman. I am fearfully helpless. And so at times, I feel nothing could be likened to her, such is her beauty.

·

I became aware of the fearful fact that nothing existed in the world except poetry. All things and all things possible are poems; from the moment language was born it has been an unspeakable truth. I wonder at the extent everyone has floundered in order to free themselves from poetry. Still it has been a most difficult discussion. Such seemingly atrocious talk.

·

When hungry, the old woman claws something from a pot and crams it in her mouth. Sometimes she takes a bath every day for three days, and sometimes she goes a month without one. Missing a ragged scrap of underclothing, she swears loudly that someone has stolen it. At the same time she will totally forget about the stock-certificates hidden under her mattress. The old

woman is reduced to pieces. Inside of that one another old woman is living.
She is exactly like those little boxes I got as a gift when a child. Inside the one
box was another one, and when you opened that one there was another one,
and even inside that box there was another smaller box . . . To get to some-
thing hidden, the old woman opens one after another, but unlike the boxes
the old woman never reaches emptiness. It is absurd to ask which is the real
old woman; she is, of course, contradictions and confusions. So the old
woman who is overly honest, I find at times extremely hateful. Because the
one laid open is me.

    •

I'm ready to be taken at anytime, says the old woman. But until I'm taken
I'm not about to die, says the old woman. Unable to take care of her own af-
fairs, she is always meddling in everybody elses'. Just leave me alone, says the
old woman. I can't say I couldn't use a little of that kind of self-respect. Be-
cause in front of the old woman I finally become me.

    •

The world is a crazy quilt. Although various colors and cloths are patched
together like insanity, the four edges are most skillfully finished. A hundred
years ago in North America there must have lived an old woman just like the
old woman. Near a large river, among beech trees, just outside a city on the
porch of a dilapidated house.

    •

Perhaps someday I too will be the old woman. Maybe I am already the old
woman. My name, my money, my future, my this and that . . . none of
these things can separate me from the old woman. My hands, my hair, my
words, my passing awareness, all the things that can be called mine and the
things of the old woman resemble each other like two eggs.

    •

Petting the belly of a dog, the old woman talks to the dog in a low voice.
The old woman delights without end in the dog's pleasure. Wondering if the
old woman would go on petting the dog for all eternity, I find I can't take my
eyes from the scene. Yet, eventually the old woman slowly stands and goes
in the house. The thing I am left with is a breathless emotion to which I can-
not, in any way, give name.

Translator's Afterword

Shuntarō Tanikawa, referred to in Japan as a "postwar poet," sensitively portrays a vision of Japan's new hope—humanitarian concerns and cosmic awareness—which more accurately places him in the company of Japan's "New Age" poets, who have abandoned the nihilism of the late forties and early fifties. He has been praised for his ability to express the attitudes and feelings of his "new generation."

An early poem, "Nero," about the death of a pet dog, published when he was twenty, reflects Tanikawa's sensitivity to humanitarian issues and his ability to elevate specifics to a universal theme:

> You know but about two summers
> I already know eighteen summers,
> and now I can remember various summers
>   both of my own and not my own:
> the summer of Maisons-Lafitte
> the summer of Yodo
> the summer of the Williamsburg Bridge
> the summer of Oran
> so I am wondering
> about the number of summers
>   that humanity has known.

Tanikawa, the only son of a philosopher and a pianist, was born in Tokyo on December 15, 1931. He was a successful student, often at the head of his class. In spite of his accomplishments and the intellectual environment of his home, he did not enjoy school.

In 1945, during the air raids on Tokyo, Tanikawa learned the lessons of war firsthand as he bicycled through the ruins of the city, viewing the charred remains of dead neighbors. His mother took him to Kyoto until the end of the war, when the family returned to Tokyo. Moving back and forth from quiet Kyoto to war-ravaged Tokyo was unsettling and he lost interest in his schooling. He later said that his greatest joy and probably only real learning during this period came from the music of Beethoven.

By the time Tanikawa was eighteen, his dislike for school was obvious. His grades began to deteriorate and he sometimes quarrelled with his teachers. He finished school by attending night classes but expressed little desire to attend college. Influenced by a friend who "liked poetry and ran off a little mimeographed magazine," Tanikawa began to read the poetry of well-known writers of this time, while, urged on by his parents, he reluctantly prepared for his college entrance exams.

A fountain pen and a monetary award gave new direction to the young man, who was uncertain what course his life would take. To study for his exams he used magazines designed as student aids. The magazines are "usually concerned with things like math and physics, but in the back there is a contributor's section, a column that includes poetry and short stories. Since I didn't want to go to college I didn't study, but occasionally I looked at the poems and stories. Those poems were bad. I felt that if I submitted something I might even win first prize. So I tried and won a fountain pen and Y3000—maybe Y1000—in cash!"

His poetry writing was still only a hobby, but during 1949 and 1950 he compiled three notebooks of his own work. His friends had left for college, and Tanikawa's father demanded to know what he planned to do. The young man wasn't sure, but in self-defense he did permit his father to look at the poetry notebooks. (Tanikawa's mother later claimed that *she* discovered the notebooks and showed them to the father.)

However the poetry came to be in the father's possession, he thought the poems showed promise. He sent the notebooks to Miyoshi Tatsuji, probably Japan's leading poet at the time. The next day, Miyoshi came to the Tanikawa house and gave his literary blessing to the boy by offering to see that several of the poems were published in *Bungakkai* (*Literary World*). "Nero" and several other poems were published in December, 1950.

After his poetry appeared in *Bungakkai*, Tanikawa was asked to write song lyrics for a composer. These lyrics proved significant to his artistic development. He found that he could receive money for his writing and that poetry was not limited to the printed pages of books and journals.

He has said that the payment for his work, instead of eliciting a sense of "gratitude," made him feel "responsible": "It was like a carpenter building a house. I was writing poetry and getting paid. It was like filling a need of the world [laughter]. I . . . had the feeling that I was offering a service to society."

Nijuoku Konen no Kodoku (*Twenty Billion Light Years of Loneliness*), his first book of poetry, was published in 1952. Tanikawa was only twenty-one, but already a prolific writer.

He recalls that "many of the poems were slipshod in form. I needed a mold into which I could pour my poetry." Having read Rilke in Japanese translation, he decided on "the sonnet form," although he really didn't understand its complexities. He thought it was a "mere line division of four stanzas of four, four, three and three lines each—that was all I knew. . . ."

A year later, he published *Rokujūni no Sonetto* (*Sixty-two Sonnets*), which further defined his sense of a cosmic consciousness—a harmony between man and his universe—and originated his own symbolism, which later critics referred to as his period of "Earth and Sky." An example of this symbolism is found in the final lines of Sonnet 45:

> By day the blue sky is telling us lies
> While night mutters the truth, we sleep
> And when morning comes we say we've dreamed.

Tanikawa explains his sky symbology:

> For me the blue sky is not the everyday sky. I see it as something extremely metaphysical. When I was young I wrote in a prose poem or someplace that in the daytime I felt enclosed by the blue sky. At night when I began to see the stars the sky was open, and I could face outwards towards the universe. Feeling closed in by the blue sky made me think that it was a symbol telling us not to consider the universe during the daytime, because mankind must be at work within society. When it becomes dark and the stars appear, man can contemplate his own existence. . . .

While associated with a group of poets whose artistic focus was the magazine *Kai* (*Oar*), Tanikawa began on his own to explore the to explore the uses of poetry in the mass media. He favored poetic drama for radio and hoped that through such writing he could return poetry "to the hands of the people." His professional and social involvement with theatre people intensified when he met and soon married Kishida Eriko, daughter of the playwright

Kishida Kunio. But he had not yet shed the only-son ties with his mother, and, as he sought to establish his personal independence and yet to make an important connection to the world of literature, his marriage felt the strains and within a year the couple was divorced.

His next major work of poetry, *Ai ni Tsuite* (*Concerning Love*), reflects his reaction to his experience of love and loss. In "Concerning a Room," he is again able to transcend his private world and approach a universal level:

> Man has surrounded himself
> space was too frightening
> time has been too sad.

Though he is concerned with his own love and the loss of it, his interest in universal themes appears in "Four Kinds of Love."

> In the first category was the love of heaven, meaning the sky and the universe. But when you look at the sky all the time, your feet are not planted on the ground. Rice and other grains are harvested from the earth, and because of the ground we are able to live. So secondly, I feel, mankind has a basic love for the earth. The third is the love for a person of the opposite sex. Of course there are homosexuals and bisexuals, but for me this means the discovery of a certain woman—just one woman, for whom there is love. Through marriage and the matter of getting along in life with that woman—somehow or other, disliking it or not—one is forced into the midst of human society. Then, for the fourth category, that man, through that woman, awakens to the love of other people; out of this love for other people develops a love of all mankind. . . .

The next few years were busy ones, both professionally and personally. In 1956, Tanikawa's *Ehon* (*Picture Book*), a volume of his own photographs and illustrative poems was published, and in 1957, Okubo Tomoko, an actress of Japan's new drama, became his second wife. A book of essays, *Ai No Panse* (*Thoughts of Love*), was published during this period. A son, Kensaku, was born in 1960, and in 1963 his daughter Shino was born.

In addition to his poetry, he found time to write a group of essays and a three-act comedy. In 1959 he wrote *Sekai E* (*To the World*) and in 1960, *Anata Ni* (*To You*). A number of the poems Tanikawa selects to read aloud at poetry readings are included in this latter work. His satirical poems on current subjects became a regular feature of the *Shunkan Asahi* (*The Asahi Weekly*) in 1961 and were eventually collected in a book, *Rakushu Kujūku* (*Ninty-nine Lampoons*), published in 1964.

Unlike many of his contemporaries, Tanikawa can utilize unexpected humor even in his serious poetry as, for example, in the last line of the title poem of *Twenty Billion Light Years of Loneliness*: "At the loneliness of twenty billion light years/Without thinking, I sneezed." Tanikawa explains, "In my own work I have had a dislike for the tragic, pathetic, and exaggerated that a lot of younger writers prefer. Even when I write exaggerated things I still hope to maintain feelings of objectivity in a sort of humorous way. . . ."

In 1964, a work of serious poetry, "21," appeared, in which the poet's talent for poetry that needs to be spoken, to be fully appreciated, is developed.

When his children were old enough to appreciate poems and stories, Tanikawa began another phase of his literary career—writing and publishing books for children. He has also made a name for himself—if not a lot of money—as the translator of the comic strip *Peanuts*.

Tanikawa was the recipient of the prestigious Record Prize for verse in 1962. In 1964, he took part in a documentary film of the 1964 Olympic Games. By the midsixties, his international reputation was secured through frequent invitations to participate in poetry festivals outside of Japan. English-language translators began to include Tanikawa in collections of postwar Japanese poetry. In 1963 he received a fellowship from the Japan Society that enabled him to spend eight months travelling in the United States and Europe. Reflections on this journey resulted in *Tabi* (*Travel*), a beautifully illustrated book of poetry published in 1968.

Tanikawa returned to the United States in April, 1970, to represent Japan at the International Poetry Festival sponsored by the Library of Congress. Praised by colleagues from the U.S. and abroad, his poems now began to appear frequently in the foreign presses.

In the following year, he returned to the United States, this time to participate in a seminar and reading of contemporary Japanese poetry at the invitation of the Asian Literature Program and the Academy of American Poets. He was joined by fellow poets Tamura Ryuichi and Katagiri Yuzuru. A bilingual reading at the Guggenheim Museum resulted in a Japan Society recording entitled *Three Japanese Poets* with Gary Snyder and myself reading the English translations. During this visit to the States, Tanikawa gave a special reading at the Association of Asian Studies meeting in Washington, D.C., sponsored by the Asian Literature Program.

Tanikawa's bilingual readings in the United States have helped to change contemporary misconceptions regarding modern Japanese poetry. During his first visits to the United States in the sixties, he found that audiences considered Japanese poetry synonymous with haiku. At first through interpreters, and later through his growing familiarity with the English language, he was able to acquaint audiences with the history of the modern Japanese poem, which began to take form in the 1880s. Influenced by numerous translations from European languages and by Japanese modernization, poets then broke away from the traditional thirty-one syllable *tanka* and the seventeen-syllable haiku to create a verse form more expressive than the shorter traditional forms. European-influenced schools quickly developed, including the Romantics, Naturalists, Proletarians, Futurists, and Dadaists, although many of the earlier attempts were still limited to alternating lines of five and seven syllables and still retained something of the diction and syntax of classical Japanese verse.

By the second decade of the twentieth century, such poets as Hagiwara Sakutaro had perfected a "spoken language free verse," which became the main vehicle for poetic expression. Many of Tanikawa's bilingual readings began with a sampling of the older poets whose language and form had influenced the shape of his own work. Nonetheless, in terms of influence from traditional to the contemporary mode of Tanikawa's poems, it is difficult to observe a real line of poetic descent. Tanikawa credits Beethoven as the strongest influence on his early writing. Although he has read most of the well-known poets who preceded him, including his teacher and benefactor Miyoshi Tatsuji, he claims that "there were no really 'great' poets who had much influence on me." However, *senryu*, light, humorous poetry popular from the seventeenth through nineteenth centuries, did influence his earliest poetry, as "they were close to my own temperament."

Later, he began to explore the works of such poets as Rilke, Jacques Prévert, Jules Supervielle, and Lorca. Other Western writers he acknowledges as having a direct influence on his work include "Albert Camus and Max Picard and the plays of Jean Giraudoux, Luigi Pirandello and Eugene Ionesco. I've read most of Hemingway and Graham Greene and like them, but have read only one of Dostoevski's novels—and somehow, I never read Marx and Freud." His Christian mother's influence can be seen most directly in his "angels" and "God" imagery of his earlier poems. Another side to this poet, whose influences range from Beethoven to Camus, is the strong impression made by "cowboy movies."

Perhaps it had to do with my being an only child and feeling isolated. I had no brothers or sisters, and I was still in junior high school during World War II. After the defeat, all the values that the Japanese had believed in were completely destroyed. It was a period of a kind of vacuum for us, and nobody knew what to believe. Many of my generation who went to college became involved in various political movements, but I didn't go to college and so remained rather isolated from the political activities of my peers. In the Western movies, I found a position with which I could sympathize. I felt great excitement when a man would go to the frontier. First, he would go all alone. He would find his own land, plant crops, build a house, get a cow and then send for his wife and children. In this way, long before thoughts of society, a person would begin to live alone out on the last land of the West— under the blue sky.

For Tanikawa, the poet who has explored traditional writings, but has carved his own niche as an adventurous modern poet open to a world filled with strong visual imagery, the Western or cowboy movie relates directly to his period of "Earth and Sky" symbolism.

In the seventies, his prodigious output continued. Some of his more important works include *Utsumuku Seinen* (*The Downcast Boy*), 1971; *Kotoba Asobiuta* (*Word Play-Songs*), 1973; *Teigi* (*Definition*), 1975; *Sonohoka ni* (*Something Else*), 1979, and *Kokakora Ressun* (*Coca-Cola Lesson*), 1981.

Other works during the last decade include numerous children's books, poetry picture books, and a best-selling translation of Mother Goose. He has published a number of Japanese nursery rhymes, his poems have been included in textbooks for young children, and he has published poetry or children's verse in nearly every magazine or journal in Japan

"Like a business man," he goes each morning to his studio-office in a plush office building in Shinjuku to spend most of his day writing. To write something every day is an obsession with him, he admits. He still composes song lyrics, is a major advocate of poetry readings—even to jazz—and has even been known to shout his poetry via bullhorn from the windows of office buildings.

His advocacy of poetry readings and his reputation as a public speaker keep his evenings as busy as his days. Recently he travelled to Nagoya in central Japan to speak to a group of nurses and social workers on the oral presentation of literature for the blind.

Today, more than thirty years after he entered a poetry contest because he didn't want to study for his college entrance exams and went on to become one of Japan's best known contemporary poets, Tanikawa feels he can finally claim to be "a real poet." He finds pleasure in a generation of "New Age" readers who feel that his humanism parallels their own contemporary vision. His output continues to be, even for him, "embarrassingly high." When pressed for the actual number of books he has written, he states firmly that he doesn't know. But then he adds, with a smile, that it is "probably a disgusting number!"

H. W.